Yoganomics Sutras

on

The Transformation Proof

Nature's Panpsychist Balance,
the Moral Compass
For the Economy

Fifth Edition

CB BO

Paul V. Cornell du Houx

Polar Bear & Company
An imprint of the
Solon Center for Research and Publishing
Solon & Rockland, Maine

A major test of theories of the early universe is to account for the patterns seen in the cosmic microwave background (CMB). —Lee Smolin, PhD, Perimeter Institute for Theoretical Physics, author of *Time Reborn: From the Crisis in Physics to the Future of the Universe*

 Polar Bear & Company™
Solon Center for Research and Publishing
Polarbearandco.org, Soloncenter.org
Galleryfukurou.com

Retailers may order via Ingram, ISBN: 978-1-959112-06-8.
Contact: PO Box 311, Solon ME 04979; info@soloncenter.org.
Gallery & events: 20 Main Street, Rockland, ME 04841.
Copyright © 2024 Paul V. Cornell du Houx
Library of Congress Control Number: 2020937533
Fifth edition: paperback, 2024
Fourth edition: paperback, 2020
Third edition: paperback, 1991
Second edition: hand bound in *Round the Cape of Faith*, 1988
First edition: calligraphy by hand, hand bound, 1982

The second edition, *Yoganomics: 370 Sutras on Natural Polarities of the Economy*, was a rewrite of *Yoganomics: Pure Motion and the Law of Economic Erosion*, my earlier attempt to apply yoga to the idea of the economy as a living organism; the book has been revised to reflect the Transformation Proof.

Cover by author, showing the Kennebec River with two of the succession of "cribs" of wood and rocks. Built on the winter ice, the cribs would sink in the spring to rest on the riverbed and stand as small islands to help guide the flow of logs. Photos and illustrations by author, unless otherwise credited.

All rights reserved. No part of this book may be reproduced in any form without permission in writing from the author or publisher, except for brief quotations for critical articles and reviews.

Manufactured on durable, acid-free paper in more than one country.

Also by Paul Cornell du Houx

Unicycle,
the Book of Fictitious Symmetry and Nonrandom Truth, or the Panpsychist Asymmetry of Nature's Democratic Pi

"Very scrupulously set out. It is extremely well written and beautifully literate."
—Dr. Diané Collinson, author of *Plain English*, *Fifty Major Philosophers*, *Fifty Eastern Thinkers*, coauthor of the *Biographical Dictionary of Twentieth-Century Philosophers*

"This book contains some serious mathematics—smart, thought-provoking, and engrossing."
—William H. Barker, PhD, Professor of Mathematics, Bowdoin College, coauthor of the textbook *Continuous Symmetry: From Euclid to Klein*

"A provocative book by a serious thinker, well worth the reader's time."
—William A. Haviland, PhD, professor emeritus and founder of the Department of Anthropology, University of Vermont, coauthor of bestselling textbooks, including *Cultural Anthropology* and *Evolution and Prehistory*

What the Farmer Told the Bard,
A Novel of Erotic Panpsychism
"This rich, dense, playful novel of philosophical, historical, and metaphysical inquiry... The material is fascinating... The novel's chief attraction is Cornell du Houx's witty, daring, allusive prose... Imaginative vigor pulses through descriptive scenes in which characters encounter gods and Shakespeare's fairies... This book certainly brings fresh and unique material to the table... daring ideas and memorable prose."
—The BookLife Prize by *Publishers Weekly*

Justin Williams

That the universe is lopsided appears to be critical for our existence. It is also perhaps the greatest of the outstanding mysteries.

—Frank Close, OBE, FRS
Emeritus Professor of Physics
University of Oxford, author of
Lucifer's Legacy: The Meaning of Asymmetry

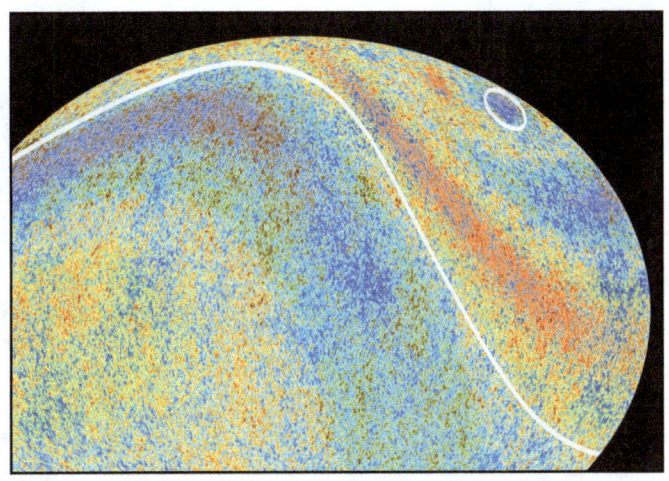

This is a cosmic microwave background (CMB) image, courtesy of the European Space Agency and the Planck Collaboration. For the full image and more information, please visit: esa.int/spaceinimages/Images/2013/03/Planck_enhanced_anomalies.

The following description accompanies the CMB image on the ESA website. While not absolute proof, this evidence of nature's asymmetry provides context for the reasoning in *Yoganomics*.

> Two CMB anomalous features hinted at by Planck's predecessor, NASA's WMAP, are confirmed in the new high-precision data. One is an asymmetry in the average temperatures on opposite hemispheres of the sky (indicated by the curved line), with slightly higher average temperatures in the southern ecliptic hemisphere and slightly lower average temperatures in the northern ecliptic hemisphere. This runs counter to the prediction made by the standard model that the Universe should be broadly similar in any direction we look. There is also a cold spot that extends over a patch of sky that is much larger than expected (circled). In this image the anomalous regions have been enhanced with red and blue shading to make them more clearly visible.

Photo Ramona du Houx

The timeless view of physics . . . has shown its impotence . . . But if we embrace the reality of time, we make possible a time-asymmetric physics within which the universe can naturally evolve complexity and structure. And thus we avoid the paradox of an improbable universe.

— Lee Smolin, PhD, Perimeter Institute for Theoretical Physics, author of *Time Reborn: From the Crisis in Physics to the Future of the Universe*

Preface

Wu wei is based on ancient ideas of pure motion, effortless action. Among its various interpretations, there are themes of symmetrical perfection, *laissez faire*, and patrician morality. Forty-five years ago, I was in my late twenties polishing my first attempt at this book, entitled *Yoganomics: Pure Motion and the Law of Economic Erosion*. I had come across some of the ideas of *wu wei* in my research, though I would not have been able to give it a name. Many practices of meditation and effortless, spontaneous action had become current by the time I was an undergraduate in economics and French in the early 1970s. And given the beguiling ubiquity of idealized motion and symmetry as modeled with calculus in economics, I was lured into a quest for reality.

Fed up with academic economics and having taken what may have been one of the last available history-of-economics courses in the United States, I decided to "launch myself from my ivory tower into the marketplace and see what most people were really doing so much of the time in their lives—at work." That was my repeated rebuttal to doubts as to why I wasn't going to graduate school. I would investigate demand and supply firsthand and write something as a result. Also, this would prove a good sequel to my grass-roots, East Coast student activism.

But once written, I increasingly treated my *Yoganomics* with the ambivalence and skepticism suitable to the whimsical portmanteau. For one thing, I had been trained to be more rigorous than to throw around words like "law" in connection with this and that.

Even so, I began to experiment with a sort of *wu wei* at work in London's business Square Mile, writing currency reports with an economics consulting firm. Then I got more down to earth with the old Price Waterhouse & Co., UK, as a dogsbody accounts auditor in a wide range of work environments. And later, in sales and marketing, in two computer companies (after a stint studying law at the Inns of Court), with a side hustle attempting a couple of start-ups (in import-export and as co-inventor of an electrical connector—long story). Eventually, there weren't many streets in London and points south where I didn't recognize a doorway of some sort in my education on the economy.

Noticeably meanwhile, *wu wei* in various guises was filtering into company training courses as the New Age got traction. So *Yoganomics* did take on a life of its own, though in unexpected ways—these old, powerful ideas have their own ways of sweeping us along, regardless.

In my academic, economics ivory tower, and given my personal background, what I had not understood was the way effortless pure motion encourages attitudes of the moneyed lifestyle.

O course, not only rich people have been attracted by the idea of an economy where money just happens most efficiently by itself—especially if you abide by a code of ethics—like a mindfully, effortlessly received income of "rents" on capital. The *wu wei* of self-righting markets that would validate your meritocracy is in fact widespread. And the belief that you can "manifest" wealth is always welcomed by many, not to overly mention the prosperity gospel.

Why didn't I know about the historic and powerful,

enduring roots of *laissez faire,* east and west? And its predictive tentacles of the obverse ethic of prideful workaholic perfectionism? One might as well ask why the economics department of such well-endowed liberal arts colleges as Amherst couldn't hold the moral high ground over admittedly well-funded forces of right-wing taboos. Why not enlighten us on the historical trail of wreckage, the centuries of suffering, left by *laissez faire* in its various formulations? As pointed out by Karl Polanyi throughout his book, *The Great Transformation* (1948), advocates of a self-regulating, *laissez-faire* economy have long toiled for governments to intervene on their behalf.

It would have been handy to know that the neoliberal Washington Consensus was being glued together with habits of thought that are finally being recognized as undergraduate "economism" or "101-ism." God forbid we should learn that the symmetrical foundation of self-righting demand-and-supply markets are a chimera that has been fought for centuries! And still needs to be opposed and shown for the self-centered, self-contradictory beast that it is, one that feeds off the poor and lower-middle classes with special appetite.

Nationwide, right-wing pressure campaigns swept away *The Elements of Economics* (1947) by Lorie Tarshis— the first economics textbook widely in circulation in the United States—as being socialist. The pseudo-Keynesian Samuelson compromise still fails to fill the void. Paul Samuelson's bestselling textbooks might claim to have enough mathematics to let the trustees of universities sleep soundly, protected by dreams of scientific neutrality in their economics departments. But the void remains.

The symmetrical demand-and-supply scissoring

of economics away from the past has left echoes that I believe many of us still feel, without being able to give them a name. The economics models developed in graduate schools still carry ingrained assumptions of utopian symmetries of prefect competition, to be crafted to fit the harsh realities of human behavior. Economists intervene in their own utopias, even as the politicians who have taken an undergraduate course or two in economism pressure democracy to let the economy leave the poor alone; they impoverish the populace with historic transfers of wealth off our backs and into the offshore accounts of heroic recipients.

Sensing the emptiness in my undergraduate economics—if not yet the abyss we all face today—I checked out the humanities for another perspective. Along with my French literature courses, I explored the anthropology department. There, I discovered cultures that had developed yoga, a name I could recognize. The liberal arts education came to my rescue. I practiced yoga and finally quit smoking. With or without causation, that was a powerful experience of addiction and illusion.

I don't know how the word "yoganomics" came to me, exactly. Grandfather Vance Dunn, an Irish Kansas farmer, popular orator and storyteller, had an entire alternative German nonsense language that he employed for the benefit of his in-laws, peppered with probable English. Plus, it was the early 1970s. Then "Reaganomics" resurrected more zombies of *laissez-faire* in the 1980s, and subsequent presidencies got burdened with the portmanteau, as the selfishness became a consensus on bootstraps and "government interference."

The Transformation Proof came to me during years

of long walks along the Kennebec River and swimming in the wild, finally to be worded into *Unicycle* by 2007.

It's true that many failed attempts have been made to connect human morality with the physical universe. What *ought* we to do when we look around us? Students of this subject are familiar with the naturalistic fallacies. We human animals have long claimed that nature has or has not a moral compass and that someone is or is not on the right side of truly awe-inspiring and often frightening realities. We are, after all, in nature, and we have various moralities. Where is the definitive dividing line, if any, between us moralizers and the rest of it?

It seemed to me that, being immersed in nature, it was only a matter of time and science before we reasoned it out. The question turned out to be more difficult than at first sight. Gods of nature have often been thought to keep empires in power. So one needs to be open to failure, in the scientific tradition.

"Panpsychism," of the curious word coined in the sixteenth century by the rebellious Francesco Patrizi, for the idea that consciousness is all pervasive, advocated by Bertrand Russell and Arthur Eddington in the 1920s—is back! A more developed treatment of the logic of asymmetry, along with illustrative stories and essays, can be found in *Unicycle*. The sequential numbers herein are a reminder of the deductive tissue, as the logic unfolds.

While the errors are mine, this edition would not exist without my wife, Ramona, who said I should rewrite *Yoganomics* and explain why. How many times have I announced to her: "It's done!"

Solon, Maine   PCdH
February, 2024

Oak leaves on solar eclipse

☙ YOGANOMICS SUTRAS ❧

1. The truth is always repeated because it can never be stated once and for all; autumn leaves repeat from one patten of color to the next, leaf to leaf, tree to tree, year after year, without ever producing the one ultimate leaf, the one tree, or the final year of all years.

2. When we stop looking for truth, speaking truth, wondering what is true, we are lost.

3. But we don't need the whole truth to find the way; we just need to care about it enough.

4. Of the various kinds of yoga, *Yoganomics* treats mind and body as being in interconnected polarities, to be stretched and relaxed, with supple care, like the yogic breathing exercises.

5. We breathe in and out with continuity and opposing polarity, where exhalation and inhalation turn into each other before the one can be perfectly identified from the other.

6. Yoga has been known to use this mystery of the absence of absolute polarities in breathing to encourage health and awareness, mindfulness.

7. Mindfulness is physically more than we think.

8. Working with yoganomics, mind and body can become a better vehicle of truth and clarity, understanding the body of the economy.

Yoganomics Sutras on the Transformation Proof

9. The main tools of yoganomics, loosely speaking, are the polarities of symmetry and asymmetry.

10. The following thought experiment will provide an introduction, to tighten things up.

11. Let's assume a perfectly symmetrical Object S (maybe pretend it's a box)—alone, all by itself.

12. Next, imagine we now have a relationship between Object S and some asymmetrical Object A—perhaps a broken box (symmetries are defined in the appendix).

13. As a result, pristine Object S can no longer be defined as being absolutely symmetrical and alone.

14. Because it is now an Object S that is in association with asymmetrical Object A; together, they form an asymmetric unity.

15. The character of S has changed by association with A.

16. The identity of S has changed.

17. The symmetry of S is in various respects broken, fractured, altered.

18. In fact, any aspect—including any physical part—of Object S we choose to observe will be in a relationship (however indirect) with asymmetric Object A and will therefore lose its pure, absolute symmetry as an object, material or otherwise.

19. The asymmetric change subtly and not-so-subtly penetrates to all parts and aspects of Object S.

20. The assumed Object S in association with Object A is now something other than the self-contained,

exclusive purity it once possessed.

21. Even so, Object S observably maintains an identity in the relationship.

22. The identity of Object S is changed but not annihilated, because asymmetry is open-ended and cannot be absolutely, symmetrically pure and final, closed off.

23. Object S can be changed but not absolutely, when it becomes asymmetric in the relationship.

24. Now this relationship between the two objects cannot both happen and simultaneously not happen.

25. By the definition of absolute symmetry, Object S is either associated with Object A or not.

26. Asymmetric Object A is not defined as being absolutely exclusive that way.

27. As soon as Object A shows up, Object S has already ruled itself out.

28. We must drop our assumption of the existence of a "perfectly symmetrical Object S (or box)," according to this proof by contradiction.

29. Asymmetry and pure symmetry are mutually exclusive.

30. If any asymmetry exists, then there can be no pure symmetry.

31. The absolutely perfectly symmetrical Object S would not happen in an environment where there are any Objects A.

32. As long as there is any question of a relationship

between any Objects S and A, Object S is preempted by any asymmetry.

33. Conversely, if S somehow happened prior to A, the asymmetry would be preempted; there would be nothing but pure, absolute S.

34. If Object S already exists, then nothing asymmetrical can find any foothold; it has no way to arise.

35. Object S in its pristine state can only endure in the absence of Object A; it could only have a prior existence, as such, in the absence of any asymmetry.

36. By observation, we know asymmetry is already pervasive in nature, in the universe.

37. So, it is "too late" for any absolute symmetry to happen, in space, time, or otherwise.

38. Furthermore, we can define pure symmetries as absolutes, and all perfect absolutes are pure symmetries.

39. Therefore, in the absence of any single pure and absolute symmetry, we are left with nature's observable, multifarious, asymmetrical pluralities and polarities.

40. In the absence of the finality of absolute symmetry, all asymmetries are connected; there is nothing to separate them absolutely, nor do they merge into pure symmetrical homogeneity.

41. This little exercise, which I call the Transformation Proof, can be unpacked in a number of ways, some of which are enumerated as follows, a more comprehensive treatment to be found in *Unicycle, the Book of Fictitious Symmetry and Nonrandom Truth*, or the *Panpsychist Asymmetry of Nature's Democratic Pi*.

Rhythmic, changing asymmetries of rock and water

42. To continue unpacking the deductive sequences with notes and corollaries here, we discover that in the absence of pure symmetry, extremely low asymmetry is often mistaken for the existence of absolute symmetry, especially in math and science.

43. In the arts, asymmetry it is too often assumed as so obvious as to merit little attention.

44. The natural asymmetries include the theoretical (albeit extremely low) asymmetries fundamental to math—we cannot meditate, think, theorize, reason or conjecture outside of nature.

45. Human animals, especially in Western cultures, have been and still are very hung up on separating mind and body, with ideas of purity of soul, purity of math and logic.

46. Curiously, the logic of asymmetry conjures fiction, where the reality of an environment in the absence of pure symmetry functions to enable us to imagine absolute symmetries and other fantasies—while building something solid.

47. Consider, for example, a number line or series of repeating units: If nature does not repeat with absolutely symmetrical exactitude, then something mysteriously creative is happening between repeats.

48. This is why we can experience repetition as rhythmically alive and musical.

49. This creativity can go so far as to build new sequencing and objects, but not without preceding patterns.

50. So science, math and the humanities need each other, need imagination, to make sense.

51. No series can repeat without nature's creative connectivity, the same connectivity that brings leaves along the branches of trees and petals round the flower, and let's not forget history—it sort of repeats.

52. So, in the absence of absolute symmetry, nature produces similarities and differences with asymmetric connectivity.

53. The most powerful physical barriers are not exempted from the logic of asymmetry.

54. When any two things connect, they must at some point, in some way, truly connect, that is, merge completely but asymmetrically.

55. Because, otherwise they will never honestly, truly, connect at all—we would be allowing for the interference of an (impossible) absolute.

56. In the absence of absolutes, nature's asymmetry allows the greatest nuance and precision.

57. Only the surface need make the slightest contact for any presumed perfect symmetry to be already broken throughout, as Object S is everywhere preempted.

58. This is true for all things; this is how consciousness flows in various physical shapes and ways.

59. Consciousness has physical, panpsychist connectivity; there is nothing beyond recognition of some kind.

60. There is no point symmetry at any beginning, ending, or in-between—no pure fulcrum of balance.

61. Nature's true balance is what is actually happening in the absence of any absolute end or beginning and in the absence of perfectly symmetrical balance.

62. Nature flows because it is never absolutely stopped.

63. Asymmetric polarity in motion takes place between order and chaos, without any absolute poles at either end.

64. There is no pure and random chaos and no perfect order along the River of Asymmetry.

65. No perfectly pure and homogeneous flow, either.

66. The more pressures build into (the absence of) a fixed, absolute pole or central position, the more counter-pressures will develop away from the impossible symmetry; this Pressure Principle flows from the proof.

67. Polarities are ever-present in asymmetric flow.

68. Nature cannot stand perfectly still.

69. Pressures for absolutes must be countered.

70. These counter-pressures may happen in the most subtle ways, near and far, or they may become violent with immediacy.

71. It is the absence of absolute dead ends that allows extraordinary subtlety and precision to develop.

72. The logic of asymmetric change improves Darwinism and deals with the theory's strange paradox of life and consciousness having to arise from mere algorithmic, biochemical operations.

73. Consciousness is asymmetric and physical.

74. It's not all a dream, nor just a machine.

75. The asymmetric quality of consciousness cannot be kept out anywhere; it is neither prior nor subsequent to matter; consciousness is connectivity.

76. Pure, absolute symmetry could not change because it would block itself from the process of unfolding connections.

77. Instantaneous change is an impossible absolute.

78. Absolute symmetry cannot inhabit untouched by the changing context of the world.

79. If pure symmetry never happens, all paradoxes are asymmetric, if only to a slight degree.

80. In order to let paradoxes live, we must let go of any absolute assumptions or ideas that absolutes exist, except in stories, fiction, art, music, and other forms of creativity.

81. The truth lets us imagine absolutes in order to understand why they cannot happen.

82. If there is no point symmetry at any beginning, ending, or in-between—no pure fulcrum of balance—then nature's true balance is what is actually happening in the absence of any absolute end or beginning and in the absence of perfectly symmetrical balance.

83. Truth exists, but it is not absolute; it is asymmetric.

84. Nature is asymmetric so it can flow.

85. We live in an asymmetric environment.

86. Yoganomics is about the mysterious but logical truth of asymmetric change and our livelihood in an economy that cannot be isolated from nature as a whole.

87. Not even so much as a paradox of equal units in a random roulette wheel of chaos marching round in near-perfect order, pure symmetry never has a chance.

88. So pure symmetry has never been found in the history of experimental science—and never will be found.

89. Pure symmetry could not survive in total isolation, because nature's asymmetries would find it out; they cannot be stopped completely, preemptively, potentially, or in any absolute way.

90. No absolute could be touched, only preempted.

91. Nature's asymmetry cannot touch anything purely symmetrically.

92. No one and nothing is so absolutely alone.

93. Nature's connective flow changes whatever it touches in many potential ways, depending on the location and context of the currents of the River of Asymmetry, the River of Life, or the Ocean of Existence.

94. The fiction highlights the truth because the truth is creative.

95. In the absence of any symmetry of perfect repetition, the River must change in creative ways, in connection with the past.

96. The creative, questioning mind can discover more about the truth; the absolutist mind repetitively jumbles chaos and order, though it can be highly skilled in its specialties.

97. The creativity generated in the absence of absolutes

allows us to tell lies and pervert the truth against nature's fundamental, asymmetric flow.

98. We all navigate the Ocean of Existence with more or less imbalance, sometimes to extremes.

99. There is no pure and perfectly absolute Yin and no such Yang in the Tao.

100. There is no absolute polarity, so nature flows, and the Tao exists.

101. We might call Yin and Yang the "non-poles" of creation.

102. By never becoming absolute rulers, by deferring to the people, they encourage nature's creative polarity.

103. To recall the Asymmetric Pressure Principle that flows from the Transformation Proof: The more pressures build into a fixed pole or central position, the more counter-pressures will develop away from the impossible symmetry, away from the place they cannot go.

104. Nature has no choice but to avoid poles of pure symmetry—perfect absolutes, perfect equilibrium.

105. Nature cannot stand perfectly still; it is the way of change.

106. Again, therefore, pressures for absolutes must be countered.

107. Nature's asymmetry is endlessly nuanced, and there is no place to stand outside of it, nor outside the livelihood of the people.

108. The creative changing connectivity of consciousness allows limits in physical objects to happen.

109. No two objects will ever be exact repetitions of each other, nor will they be entirely different.

110. There are no one-off, absolutely final, single events.

111. So nature repeats in rhythms of development, thematic patterns of repetition, waves.

112. By the logic of asymmetry, the waves never repeat absolutely exactly, never developing perfect symmetry of repetition.

113. In reality, the units of a number line cannot repeat exactly, nor can any sequence of objects; they are in this respect wavelike.

114. To conceive of them as pure symmetries is to conjure fiction somewhere in the math.

115. There are no perfect central points, no perfect circles.

116. Waves and particles can be imagined as poles apart.

117. But in the absence of absolute finalities to separate them, they must be connected.

118. So the intense pressures that build towards the symmetrical point of particle formation conjure the experience of corresponding wave formation as part of the character of the light or the wheel of pi.

119. Similarly, the more the waves repeat exactly, the more they call forth the alternative experience of particle formation in the avoidance of any absolutely exclusively symmetrical, continuous wave motion.

120. In order to exist in the reality of the natural world, all circles must have some traction.

Yoganomics Sutras on the Transformation Proof

121. There is no traction in pure perfection.

122. Every circle must be at least very slightly loose or off-center on its axis.

123. Waves have circularity around centers that move and change, connecting them in polarity with other destinations and media.

124. The number pi can only exist if it is rounded off "by hand," on purpose.

125. Pi cannot round itself off; it must be in a relationship, whether or not we know where that is.

126. Pi does not exist without being rounded off, giving life to the circle, with its central particle and waves of change.

127. In the absence of perfectly exact points of symmetry, there are asymmetric particles and dots.

128. Some dots, however defined, have extremely low asymmetry.

129. Waves often have extremely low asymmetry.

130. A normal distribution and all distributions in probability and statistics are asymmetric with tails that connect in asymmetric infinity.

131. Asymmetric infinity connects where we stop counting (see *Unicycle* for the development of this math).

132. Pi predicts that no pure symmetry will ever be found; pi can be rounded off in a creative multitude of connective ways.

133. Like all languages, math can say many things powerfully, without having to achieve perfection, and it

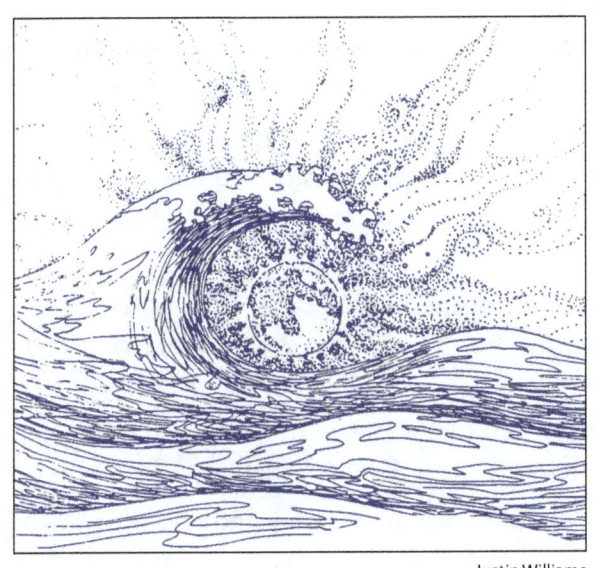

Justin Williams

Particles, waves and polarities of pi

can miss the mark in describing nature, when it assumes perfection or mistakenly embraces paradox.

134. The language of asymmetry can develop mathematically, philosophically, and in many other directions.

135. In yoganomics, we observe that nature always has process, and natural change has the balance of the relationships of true Yin and Yang.

136. In the absence of absolutes, nature must change and allow us the opportunity to discover the quality of change and how we change in the shifting balance of the flow.

137. The inspiration to discover ethical change is a matter of survival in a universe of dangerous and often incalculable forces.

138. Within the polarities of order and chaos nature is inspirational, as well as destructive.

139. We can learn to navigate and find the way to go.

140. In the absence of the discovery of universal connectivity, the scientific and philosophical search for a way to explain how the mind and perceptions of quality can be found exclusively in the functions of the brain and body will continuously fail.

141. The absolutist separation of mind and body is an age-old human tendency that has often led to artificialities and superficial judgment of quality.

142. The consequences of judgmental behavior and objectification develop economies of oppression and enslavement, overt and subtle, from religion to science, to arts and humanities, to environmental disaster.

Justin Williams

143. With the inclusion of the mind in a broader understanding, nature ever becomes a source of inspiration with objects of wonder.

144. Where nothing ever collapses into pure chaos or perfect order, there is always a tension between order and chaos, a balance that can be stormy or peaceful, like the weather.

ॐ ॐ

145. Are we contradicting ourselves by being absolute about there being no absolutes?

146. Close, sometimes, but—not really. Why?

147. First, we are finding more and varied ways of saying it, without ever finding any absolute end to nature's potentials for creative expression.

148. That is different from being absolute; being absolute would require a perfectly final statement, and no more could be said—ever—about that or anything else.

149. In addition, the absolute is disqualified from opposition; it is a conjured fiction of the imagination, as in a story, not a reality in any non-fictitious sense.

150. We cannot really be absolute about anything, for or against.

151. We can only be absolutist and fall short of the impossible destination.

152. Affirmations, deductions, can keep opening up with new possibilities.

153. The imagination is real, so it can imagine things that are not.

154. Stories are possible, because the truth exists.

155. Attitudes of absolutism are not conducive to good storytelling.

156. Absolutism tends to be blunt at the wrong time, while nature allows for the greatest precision in the ever-rebalancing rhythmic polarities of flow.

157. When we nail something, it should be part of building a project, a creative process, not just to keep nailing down some thing.

158. Nature can be creative because it has heart.

159. Creativity is not just about something new; it is about taking care in what we do, in acknowledging relationships past, present and potential.

160. Craftsmanship is creative.

161. Art is empty without care and craftsmanship.

162. Competition is empty without good sportsmanship.

ങ ള

163. Nature has a moral compass to be found: asymmetry is fundamentally non-exclusive.

164. Recall that pure symmetry and asymmetry are mutually exclusive; if pure symmetry existed, it would exclude everything but itself.

165. Also, nature's inclusiveness is not random; it is alive with a sense of direction on the River of Asymmetry.

166. Separations and differences are fundamentally united, connected.

167. That which connects us is more profound than the differences that divide us.

168. The fact that nature's asymmetry is multifarious and fundamentally inclusive is a moral fact.

169. This fact provides the ethical basis for a democratic society and a fresh understanding of natural law.

170. The fundamental connection we feel with nature is empathy.

171. The cultivation of a natural sense of value in the absence of judgmental absolutism calls for curiosity and caring in polarity between oneself and others, including the environment and beyond.

172. There is a natural polarity in relationships, between coming together and falling apart.

173. The closer we are to the heartbeat of the River, the more our differences can delight us and bring us together.

174. For the River has many different rhythms and the love of many souls.

175. In the absence of the absolute finality of pure symmetry, nature ensures that death is not final; it's the way of change.

176. And in the absence of any symmetrically absolute, one-off unrepeated events, we should credit cultures that regard the rhythms of reincarnation as a reality.

☙ ❧

177. There is no perfect love that beats like a single heart for all.

178. In the absence of absolutes, there is a natural polarity between oneness and plurality, between mythologies of one god and many gods.

179. A balance in community can be found in the adherence to a monotheism that cares about providing opportunities to the people, in polarity between one and the many.

180. Absolutism is an addiction that finds excuses wherever it can, whether it be among the many gods or in one god.

181. Absolutism is the addiction to power and money, so we need to be clear about what we mean by capitalism.

182. Because markets are asymmetrically capable of great nuance in discovering and fulfilling requirements, capitalism can become a religion of addiction.

183. Addiction is the inability to let go of the circle that will never close with perfection, leaving one with increasingly unfulfilled desire, gripping a wheel of fire.

184. In the absence of absolutes, the River of Asymmetry must keep moving, and the tension involved might seem as though it must somehow be resolved in universal powers of nature or in something supernatural or in greater wealth.

185. Often we pray to mythical powers for resolution.

186. But the River moves towards chaos, and the river moves towards peace, and neither is completely resolved, while the wonderful tension continues in so

many ways as to enthrall the imagination and inspire the poets, the musicians, the listeners, the animals, all who live by the River and hear the pipes of Pan.

187. But the tension in nature's sense of direction can be too much, and sometimes we buckle and cave and crave resolution, absolutism.

188. The addict keeps coming back to the roulette wheel in some form or other, in a bottle, in a pill, in a religious obsession.

189. Children are born addicted in poisoned environments, where the economy has gone mad in the worship of money and power, depriving the people of universal health care, exposing humanity to wild changes in the climate.

190. Addiction can be spread through chemical and social means, transmitted to the innocent.

191. Obsessions take hold, as we double down, again and again, fixated with enclosing the circle of control on Nature herself.

192. We are learning how stress reverberates throughout the body, activating the endocrine system in ways that amount to behavioral and chemical addiction when relieved in cycles of fulfilled and unfulfilled craving.

193. Absolutism generates and lives off physical feedback, reinforcing even exquisite pleasures, where successes, victories more or less genuine, are exaggerated and distorted with illusions of being "on a roll" in the River of Life or simply feeling normal again.

194. Why do we randomly gamble when we know the

house always wins the long game? When we know the casino that contains the slot machines is the standing evidence that we are basically losers if we think we can win so big?

195. The way to participate in roulette is to know it's about participation—not just winning—to realize we are paying for the fun of it, for the occasion, which is fair enough, if that's what we like, unless we overspend.

196. Capitalism functions while prone to excessive competition accompanied by the paranoia of addiction, lurching from and torn between many polarities.

197. Dysfunctional, unbalanced capitalism is caught in cyclical polarities of over- and under-consumption, adverse demand, over- and under-investment, inefficient production, polluted supply, extremes of wealth, power, and poverty, to name a few.

198. In order to rebalance the flow, we need to learn to live within the tension in the powers of nature and not be too afraid.

199. The surfing analogy—where the wave breaks and the skill of the surfer merges with nature's breaking asymmetric circles of smooth curves and bubbles of turbulence and foam—provides inspiration in the dance of the absence of absolutes.

200. There are many kinds of flow, from whitewater rafting to gliding downstream with a six-pack or a bottle of wine, all of which can provide inspiration and relaxation, release of tension.

201. The harmony of asymmetric motion can be found in the beauty of sailing, flying, windmills.

202. There is flow in being at one with one's work.

203. The experience of flow can wake us up—or lull us to sleep when we turn away from the challenges of ensuring human rights, remuneration according to real value, genuine quality and care, fair trade.

204. We need to build a better sense of community along the River, in nature, where it is safer and love can flourish with the natural power to deal with challenges.

205. We need enjoyable markets and town squares and a good street life, where quality in a wide range of goods and services is appreciated as creative, awakening the senses, strengthening a positive, hopeful outlook.

206. We need to stand up and demand good money for good work.

207. We need to balance the inevitable universal potentials for addiction in us all with organized labor to negotiate on behalf of workers and with community support through representative government.

208. Nature's asymmetric inclusiveness encourages us to work together to overcome what Chris Hayes describes in *Twilight of the Elites* as excessive "social distance" where: "The obsession with rank reflects deep cultural anxiety over and simultaneous addiction to the ceaseless war for top status, the never-ending treadmill of competition and achievement that we've set as our ideal (Crown, Kindle Edition, p. 163)

209. Elitism is addictive to rich and poor alike in the development of social hierarchies of power, where the poor lose the ability to properly judge the rich.

210. People who are stressed and stretched to the limit, working two or three jobs, in a society lacking community spirit, find it extremely difficult to realize that vastly unbalanced inequality of wealth means that the rich folks (not the poor) have got your money.

211. To repeat: In the absence of absolute finality, universal connection overrules absolute divisions; it's natural law.

212. We must relearn what our ancestors intuited in past millennia: If Nature lives in our bodies, beats with our hearts, she must also think with our brains and bodies in a polarity of shared consciousness.

213. In order to have the moral authority to demand a civilized distribution of economic value, we must

Public domain, via Wikimedia Commons

By Vincent van Gogh, overpowered by frame.

cultivate an empathetic relationship with the River of Life and share in its democratic flow.

214. People in need have been shamed into believing that the rebalancing of the flow of wealth in the economy through democratic government in their favor is somehow a "handout" or a "leg up," when it is not; it is their civic duty to claim what is rightfully theirs in order to help ensure the health of their community and their country.

215. The more that community spirit develops, the easier it becomes to know who has benefited enough and who is still in need, as society is progressively healed along with the environment.

216. This is the humbling thought: that not only is the earth not the center of the universe (the article of faith not so long ago), but we are not the most aware creatures in the cosmos, nor the most civilized, surely.

217. To assume otherwise is like assuming one has no ego of addiction—trapped in a mundane outlook on life, eventually a cog in a hierarchical machine, cosmic wheels within wheels, going nowhere malevolently, to paraphrase Aldous Huxley.

218. Given the revelations of our current science about other planets and the way we have treated this planet, to think we are the apex of civilization in the universe can now be considered self-centered, or worse.

219. This need not have us worshiping in idolatry ancient hierarchies of gods who personify the forces of nature, but there is a balance where we simply recognize that no absolute, final dividing lines disconnect our awareness from the rest of the universe.

Photo Ramona du Houx

The Green Man

220. There is an interconnected consciousness in all environments that ensures the possibility of a greater understanding, a godlike immersion of many different kinds in the world from before the earth's formation.

221. This panpsychist vision is ancient.

222. In Japanese tradition, the potter, the artist, will likely recognize the vital significance of imperfection in connective balance, in the absence of absolutes, as in kintsugi.

223. Many world views and belief systems past and present are under-appreciated in the cultural dominance of overreaching monotheism, empowered by colonialism and the misfortunes of war.

224. But we can now reasonably speculate that if the whole of nature is alive and cannot be one absolute being, then manifold cultures inhabit regions near and far among the stars and that we are invited to discover the River of Life where we live, and to be aware of the subtleties of addictive absolutes.

225. This kind of speculation must be admissible in discussing the economy, or we are doomed to be regarded as mere "agents" of an empty materialism and runaway, meritocratic capitalism, where value is thought to come from the exclusivity of sheer competition, instead of from the River of Life that runs through the asymmetric economy.

226. Institutional "theft" by monopoly and oligarchy, like systemic racism, is generated by the creeping usurpation of true value in the economy, resulting in the conditions described by Matthew Desmond in *Poverty, by America*.

227. Economists have long searched for a workable understanding of value in order to categorize and evaluate the relationships of the marketplace.

228. Without a sense of true value, it is impossible

to analyze economic activity or know the value of a currency, the value of work, of goods and services, of bastions of economic power, even of categorical definitions, like private property.

229. To the extent that there are illusions about value in the economy, nature will find them out, because all markets are inseparable from the changing asymmetric environment and human behavior therein.

230. Absolutism in attitudes concerning the value of people and things will build pressures that will back up on the economy and discredit the currency.

231. The simplistic definition of individuals in economics as "agents," ignoring the possibility of the soul in the subtlety of human experience, encourages the objectification of people and their relationships.

232. Ironically, the utilitarian marginalism of mainstream economics today basically assumes these agents to be omniscient gods, in order for mathematical models of the economy to identify fundamental value as mere prices of goods and services, land, labor, and money, thereby equating one's wage or salary with the value of one's self.

233. In order for markets to clear with symmetrical perfection, where all so-called demand is perfectly supplied, now or in future, all agents must have perfect knowledge of the economy and its universal environment.

234. Otherwise mistakes in evaluation will of course be made market-wide, leaving unmet demand and oversupply, money valued at the wrong rates of interest,

causing excessive inflation or deflation, unemployment, along with the many familiar social misfortunes.

235. In order to make their versions of this model of the self-clearing, self-regulating market work, influential economists have gone so far as to claim that the unemployed *choose* not to work, as though the jobless are gods on vacation with off-world wealth.

236. For how can such a standard of "true value" be whatever the market will bear in pricing an object—human or otherwise—unless all market behavior is divinely omniscient?

237. Although aspects of the economy can be evaluated, ultimately the value of the economy cannot be priced—that's nature's "free lunch," abused time and again.

238. As interest rates are the price of money and money is the measure of the value of the economy, then there is no perfect rate of interest at any time.

239. Markets do not just "tend towards equilibrium" and clear with absolute symmetry, where some vast and divinely offered supply meets perfectly measured human demand.

240. In the absence of well-valued investments by a democratic government that represents the actual people, the assumption of perfect economic symmetry leads to actions that pollute the real relationships of the marketplace.

241. While most economists accept that markets are not perfect, they still begin by assuming perfection and try to make adjustments in the hope that economic models will usefully predict outcomes of human behavior.

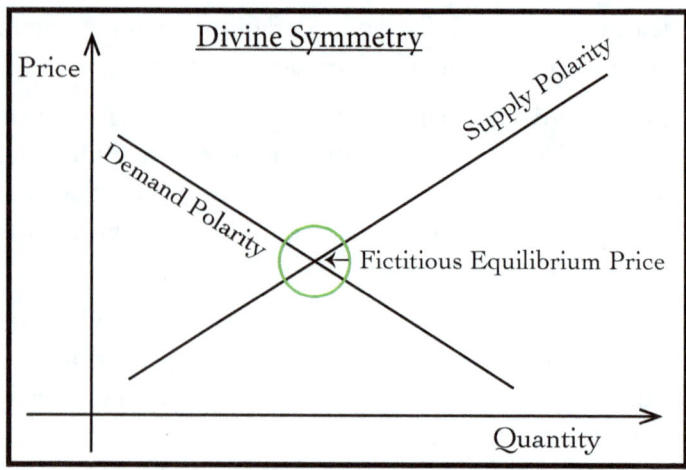

Fig. 1. *The mythical assumption that demand and supply always tend towards a perfect equilibrium price to map a mythical economy of self-regulating markets that are damaged by almost any government "intervention" reinforces capitalist illusions.*

242. Most of us recognize that we wear different hats at different times: sometimes we are in the market to buy something and sometimes we are at work helping to supply goods and/or services.

243. We personally live in shifting polarities of many different kinds, some of which involve markets more closely than others.

244. In the chapter entitled "The Magic of the Marketplace" in his book, *Economism: Bad Economics and the Rise of Inequality*, James Kwak succinctly describes how forces of demand and supply so often move so as to provide signals in the form of prices that guide decisions that give markets their power and flexibility.

245. Figure 1 shows the basic ingredients for the rea-

soning as to how markets might move in the direction toward one pole, that of "equilibrium price."

246. Prof. Kwak (yes, let the levity subside) then provides a quote from Paul Samuelson's textbook, *Economics* (p. 38), positing John D. Rockefeller's dog who gets the milk that an impoverished child would have had, if demand and supply hadn't delivered it to the rich man with symmetrical exactitude of price.

247. The dog gets the milk because supply and demand deliver to those who pay the highest price, sort of like an auction—but what is not part of the narrative in economics is that the more supply and demand pressure towards a symmetrical "equilibrium price," the more nature will build pressures *away* from that pole, because all equilibrium is asymmetric.

248. What, therefore, do markets pressure towards

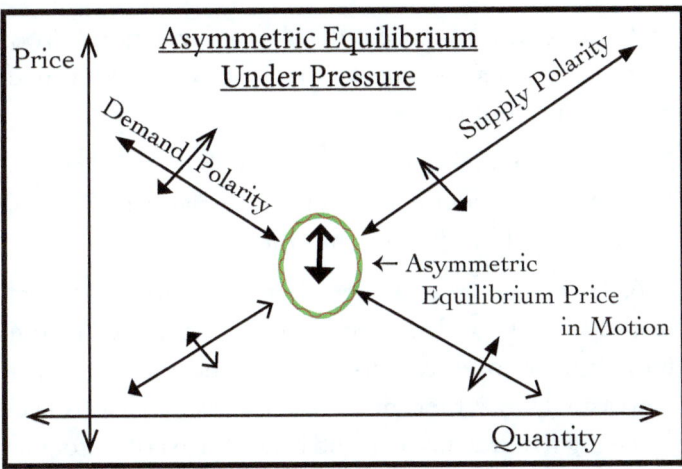

Fig. 2. *The more pressures build toward the impossible pole of absolute symmetry, the more pressures must build away from the non-existent, perfect center.*

when they move away from the idealized equilibrium of the symmetries of textbook mythology?—chaos?

249. Between the utopian pole of symmetrical intersection and the fearsome pole of pure chaos, we can navigate an asymmetric, democratic equilibrium.

250. The more we move towards a healthy democracy, the more prices reflect the true value of goods and services and the less fictitious they become.

251. In a society suffering from excessive inequality, the rich lose track of value; what is inflation to them?

252. Inflation in fact means you can't afford the price!

253. "Equilibrium price" and the mythical self-righting economy have long become a fixation, even an addiction, that drives so much of the world's misery by stopping —in the name of math and science—vital government help on behalf of the community.

254. As deduced from the Transformation Proof, asymmetric change means that nature is never fixed with finality, but is always on the move.

255. If democratic government fails to correct the market, the rudderless forces of demand and supply will run the ship of state onto the rocks.

256. If the people are in denial of their communal, civic responsibility to elect good leaders, they are handing money over to elites, monopolies, and oligarchs, who increasingly lose their moral compass in a vicious cycle wheeling towards fascism and other forms of autocracy.

257. Markets will never clear at any equilibrium of demand and supply to solve this human challenge.

258. James Kwak provides the reasoning used by advocates of so-called self-regulating markets as to why equilibrium prices supposedly bring us optimum social benefits.

259. The reasoning with your consumer hat on is that anyone who would have paid more than the equilibrium price gets a social benefit (called "consumer surplus") equal to the difference between what they would have paid and the equilibrium price they paid.

260. With your supplier hat on, your benefit ("producer surplus") is the difference between the equilibrium prices you sold your goods or services at and the lower prices you would have been able to accept.

261. The deceptive term for the sum of consumer and producer surplus is "social welfare," which can even be pseudoscientifically demonstrated with calculus.

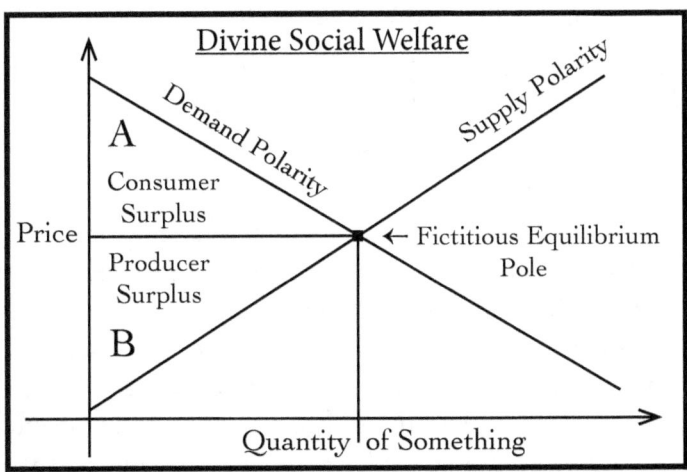

Fig. 3. *Consumer surplus + producer surplus = social welfare. What is wrong with this picture?*

262. Are we getting social welfare because we didn't have to pay more? and because we didn't have to accept a lower price?—better than two slaps about the face with a wet fish?

263. What sorts of pressures are there for symmetrical equilibrium from folks with many hats, so that money does change hands?—a haggle in the souk? some wheeling and dealing over the sticker price of a vehicle?

264. In Figure 3, Triangle A contains everyone with a buyer's hat who has haggled the price down towards the fictitious equilibrium pole below the price they might imagine they would have paid if pressed harder (folks below the demand line get some "consumer surplus," depending on where they are inside the triangle).

265. In Triangle B, it's the supplier hats who are assumed to get "producer surplus" (again, no cash on the barrel head), because they figure they could have provided more for less than the agreed equilibrium price.

266. Assuming we are all haggling over margins, everybody supposedly gets social welfare—except for those folks who are not suppliers (like no job) or haven't enough money to be in the market.

267. But among those with an income and perhaps a real job, economism dictates that everyone is hounding after the best deal, where money changes hands after all the bargaining and competition, where we all settle on an exact quantity sold at the symmetrical equilibrium sticker price . . . and thereby hangs a tale of connected counter-pressures—life is messy, as we know, and this asymmetry can come home to bite us in the ass.

268. What's the story with our purchasing habits, anyway?—got to have one 'cause everyone does? how's the strength of the marketing department? are we just buying a brand?—do we really need this? what about the environmental footprint? what illusion, what myth are we buying into? what quantity of what goods and services are we really purchasing? entire supply chains?

269. As many salespeople will tell you, a price has its story.

270. What other pressures are there, assuming everyone isn't just out for the money—if we have soul.

271. Let's not forget our hats.

272. Under the sometime pressures of the hat that asks what and how much to buy at what price, we might keep a lookout for a bargain, whereas under the worker's hat we might hope the company gets the best possible price for the security of our jobs—herein members of the community are potentially very stressed and alienated from ourselves.

273. The more competitive we all are, chasing the money, the more we are self-contradicting ourselves: which do we want, a higher price or a lower price?

274. The more competitive we are, not looking out for each other, the more self-centered and perfection-oriented we become, and the more fictitious are the prices, the weaker the signals from prices as to where and how much to invest, to produce, to innovate, as to what is needed and where true value is, and we lose the ability to know what we should be paid and therefore the confidence to demand a fair wage—confidence!

275. The tighter the tension on prices in the paradox of the symmetry of demand and supply, the more nature will untie the knots in the economy with potentially catastrophic results; that's what Figures 1-3 basically show.

276. And lets not forget that each price has the backstory of all the goods and services that went into its creation, so that it dissolves into complexity the more you look at its true nature.

277. Likewise, demand, desire has a complex psychological backstory; price and quantity are not absolute.

278. The fact is, nature—including the economy—tends *away* from equilibrium, even as it closes in on any non-existent absolute pole of equilibrium price.

279. Recall that by the logic of the Pressure Principle, nature is always in motion; we need to find the real balance of asymmetric economic equilibrium.

280. History should be required in economics courses to alert us to addictive economism, and give perspective on how such a simplistic and soulless philosophy as utilitarianism could usurp the imagination and be used to calculate the value we might place on consuming even more, especially when combined with math to be claimed as scientifically apolitical—the "marginal utility" of having just one extra unit of something.

281. The demand line usually goes downward and the supply line upward based on how "useful" one additional unit supposedly is when calculated under supplier and buyer hats.

282. Is it worth it to offer an extra unit of something at a particular price?—as the price you can get rises, so

goes the quantity you are willing to gear up for and sell, so goes the narrative.

283. As the price rises, the buyer hats shy away, and the demand line falls, fast or slowly in some curve, accordingly—plausibly, up and down, in the abstract.

284. At the intersection of the demand and supply curves is the price dot of point-symmetry fame.

285. Even if companies have a real grasp on their costs and pricing strategy, given the expected changing market conditions, who on earth goes around with a buyer's hat on and a magic calculator continuously refreshing their preferences at different prices?

286. Not to overly stress that as a community we are

The tide is out on the Blackwater River in Southern Ireland, with nature's asymmetric, rhythmic flow. I built this 17-foot daysailer with many scraps, a few purchases, and of course love—priceless! Sailing is all about the balance of asymmetric pressures and polarities of wind and water.

often conflicted people, hoping for both more *and* less.

287. This is one reason why the law of contracts exists, with a long history of trying to agree and get along, be civilized about the human costs and prices of things.

288. The healthier the community, the better the law and the more accurate the price, as they all tell a truer story, instead of false expectations and fears of falling short.

289. Sutra 114 referenced units as being wavelike; prices have flow in the fulfillment of agreements, as monetary value changes hands and moves on, while goods and services move accordingly, rivers of exchange—or the movement might remain in abeyance, as potential exchanges, "sticky prices," or as congested supply chains.

290. Prices are multifaceted and asymmetric symbols in the language of the economy.

291. Yet there is a chorus of academic voices in the Quixotic quest for symmetry, as evidenced in this quote from *Symmetry: A Very Short Introduction* by Prof. Ian Stewart, showing how he fiddles the distinction of "symmetry" and thereby avoids addressing what is in fact extremely low asymmetry (my italics below):

> Of course, symmetry in living creatures is never perfect. Mathematical symmetry is an idealized model. However, slightly imperfect symmetry requires explanation; it's not enough just to say "it's asymmetric". A typical asymmetric shape would be *very different* from its mirror image, not almost identical. (OUP, Kindle Edition, p. 90)

292. Ian Stewart seems keen to fudge the vital and well-

established issue of asymmetry: "A typical asymmetric shape would be very different"; asymmetry is relegated to big differences, and extremely low asymmetry is therefore defined out of the picture, allowing Stewart the space to describe nature as symmetrical.

293. Ian Stewart's Amazon.com biographical sketch says that he is emeritus professor of mathematics at the University of Warwick and a leading popularizer of mathematics; author or coauthor of over 200 research papers on pattern formation, chaos, network dynamics, and biomathematics; Fellow of the Royal Society and served on its governing body; has five honorary doctorates; published more than 120 books.

294. Human attachment to absolutes, as exemplified in Prof. Stewart's biographical credits, is deep and abiding; a search of his entire book, *Symmetry*, yields only about a dozen references to asymmetry and none in the index.

295. As Prof. Rhonda Garelick observes in her *New York Times* article, *When Did We Become So Obsessed With Being 'Symmetrical'? A slew of filters on social media allow users to evaluate their features, reigniting age-old obsessions with perfection and beauty:*

> The human fascination with symmetry is an ancient phenomenon, with vast cultural and biological implications, which helps explain the strong emotions being expressed on social media. Beauty has always invited quantification and assessment. Aristotle believed that "the chief forms of beauty are order and symmetry." Vitruvius, architect of the ancient Roman world, compared the beauty of a symmetrical temple to

the beauty of a symmetrical person. Leonardo da Vinci created his famous "Vitruvian Man" drawing in 1490, representing a nude human figure of ideal and symmetric proportions, demonstrating the mathematical constraints posited by Vitruvius, known as the "golden ratio." . . . But isn't it rather soulless to reduce our singular, precious faces to equations and ratios? What about the charm of imperfection? Drew Barrymore's adorably crooked smile? Ellen Barkin's sexy off-kilter features? Cindy Crawford's mole?*

296. Fortunately, nature's asymmetries, including good science and technology, are upending conventional wisdom: witness the unexpected asymmetries in the cosmic microwave background (CMB) or the early-universe galaxies that were assumed to be random, now revealed as rhythmically varied by the James Webb Space Telescope.**

297. The Federal Reserve in the US and central banks worldwide may do their best to adjust interest rates (price of money) to offset perceived and expected distortions

---

*Rhonda Garelick is the D.E. Hughes Jr. Distinguished Chair for English at Southern Methodist University and author of *Mademoiselle: Coco Chanel and the Pulse of History*. www.nytimes.com/2022/08/23/style/is-your-face-symmetrical.html.

**esa.int/spaceinimages/Images/2013/03/Planck_enhanced_anomalies.
www.nytimes.com/2024/01/05/science/space/astronomy-galaxies-bananas.html?action=click&module=editorContent&pgtype=Article&region=CompanionColumn&contentCollection=Trending.

in the economy, inflation and unemployment, but the representative body of the community must do its duty and help build social justice, environmental justice—otherwise the economy will be essentially rudderless, at the mercy of the asymmetric Pressure Principle.

298. Ethical community-building judgments must be made by the central government and all governmental bodies, based on reason and statistical evidence, with an empathetic understanding of quality, nature's true value.

299. Money must be invested judiciously by representative government for the health and security of the economy.

300. To quote Prof. Dani Rodrik in *Economics Rules: The Rights and Wrongs of the Dismal Science* (2015):

> Today, economists are increasingly turning their attention to markets in which consumers do not behave fully rationally [like idealized gods]. This reorientation has produced a new field called behavioral economics, which attempts to integrate the insights of psychology with the formal modeling approaches of economics . . . We have moved beyond competitive models to imperfect competition, asymmetric information, and behavioral economics. Idealized, flawless [symmetrical] markets have given way to markets that can fail in all sorts of ways. Rational behavior is being overlaid with findings from psychology. Typically, the expansion has its roots in empirical observations that seem to contradict existing models. (W. W. Norton & Company, Kindle Edition, pp. 68-70)

301. However, Dani Rodrik reminds us that "the grandiosely titled First Fundamental Theorem of Welfare Economics is probably the crown jewel of economics" (*Economics Rules*, p. 47).

302. The *laissez-faire* economics of the eighteenth century and its delusions of self-regulating markets cycled back as neoliberalism or the Washington Consensus after a historical succession of disasters discrediting it (as described by Karl Polanyi in his enduring book, *The Great Transformation: The Political and Economic Origins of Our Time*); the Great Recession of 2008 caused a rethink, but the *laissez-faire* ego will always try to close the circle.

303. The obsession with symmetries of absolutism in various guises cannot be assumed to go away anymore than the human ego will give up trying to control nature.

304. Dani Rodrik continues to emphasize that still,

> First-year doctoral students typically spend their first semester building up to a proof of this [Invisible Hand] theorem, picking up a fair bit of mathematics (real analysis and topology) along the way that most will never use again. The [First Fundamental] theorem is nothing more than a mathematical statement of a key implication of . . . the "perfectly competitive market model." It says, in brief, that a competitive market economy is efficient. More precisely, under the stated assumptions of the theorem, the market economy delivers as much economic output as any economic system possibly could. There is no way to improve on this outcome, in the sense that no reshuffling of resources could possibly leave some-

one better off without making some others worse off. Note that this definition of efficiency—Pareto efficiency, named after the Italian polymath Vilfredo Pareto—pays no attention to equity or other possible social values: a market outcome in which one person receives 99 percent of total income would be "efficient" as long as that person stands to lose from any income reshuffle . . . If today we associate markets readily with efficiency, it is largely because of more than two centuries of—let's not beat around the bush—indoctrination about the benefits of markets and capitalism (p. 47).

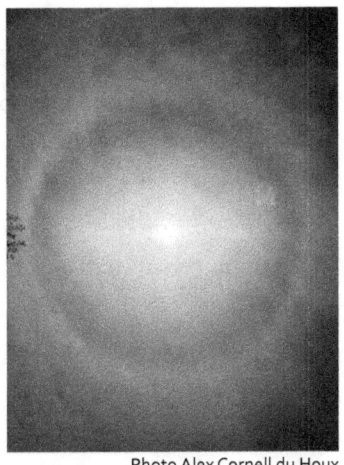

Photo Alex Cornell du Houx

Asymmetries of pi and a Hunter moon

305. The so-called efficiencies of the symmetry-based First Fundamental Theorem of Welfare Economics that is the basis of the brief analysis in the foregoing sutras and diagrams are against nature to the extent that they have invited some of our worst angels to "pay no attention to equity or other possible social values" and bring on mayhem and the ongoing destruction of the planetary environment.

306. This brings us to the psychology of ego and power, something most economists have been reluctant to face until recently.

307. A working definition of "ego" is simply a weakness for absolutes, which is easily confused with valuing an understanding of absolutes in storytelling.

308. The assumption that you have no ego is the warning light of the soul.

309. The demands of the addicted are typically supplied by the pusher; unbalanced markets and bubbles develop, while natural forces reveal the absence of any symmetrical equilibrium, whether fixed or in flow.

310. Nature's moral compass is accessible to all; it is multifaceted, variegated like a river, always moving in some preferred direction in asymmetric equilibrium.

311. But if nature is moving with organic minds of many individual motivations, present and accounted for as well as unknown, let's further explore how the fundamental connectivity and inclusiveness encouraged along the River of Asymmetry is basically good.

312. We can deduce from the Transformation Proof that in the absence of absolute finality, asymmetric consciousness is open-ended and empathetic by nature.

313. We might add that the empathetic and even loving openness is specific to the context, in that it can't be random.

314. So we are not being coerced into a club.

315. But an omnipresent, physical consciousness can sound ominous.

316. What about polarized consciousness?

317. It's safe to say that love is not absolutist, judgmental, and fundamentally exclusive towards others.

318. And love is about more than just one's self; we love in polarities of relationships with others.

319. To practice self-centeredness is a symmetry of psychological weakness leading to a loss of self and identity, a loss of a sense of direction in life.

320. The self is not indestructible; it increasingly comes apart without the balance in polarity with others and its universally living environment.

321. We need community—but of what kind?

322. Good and healthy communities work for multiracial democracy and defend it against monoculturalism.

323. The moral compass is instinctive in the soul, but it becomes congested by ego.

324. Awareness of the unfair polarity of rich and poor is a salient way to access one's moral compass.

325. Nature's moral compass takes many shapes, but they all show the way of the heart of the River of Asymmetry in action.

326. Empathetic action is guided by nature's moral compass specifically to prioritize the liberation of life pressured under conditions of low asymmetry to rebalance unfair polarities of wealth and health.

327. At either end of the polarity of rich and poor,

illusions have formed like a weather system round the empty pole.

328. The rich lose track of who they are and become susceptible to paranoid ideas about their image in society, and they increasingly fear and oppress "the people," consciously or not—unless they can keep track of their moral compass and work to rebalance the polarity of rich and poor, so no one is poor.

329. Unfair inequality means that the rich have wealth that should naturally belong to the rest of society—bluntly stated, unbalanced markets have given them other people's money.

330. The dead end of poverty is a near symmetry of absolute oppression, of working paycheck-to-paycheck, if you have a job or two or three, none of which pays enough, stretched to the limit, with bleak prospects for the next generation—a psychological and often physical, homogeneous wasteland.

331. In this nightmare, it is extremely difficult to keep track of your moral compass, and it can be nearly impossible to understand democracy as a reason to reclaim the wealth that has been wrongly redistributed to the rich.

332. Poverty, like undue wealth, can easily promote delusions of autocracy.

333. So what is fair?

334. It used to be recognized that good business has a responsibility to the community, not just the shareholders.

335. Community happens the more we employ nature's open-ended opportunities for all by prioritizing those most in need.

336. That's democracy.

337. The founders of the United States hoped and assumed that there was such a thing as "nature's law," for the people, as stated in the Declaration of Independence.

338. The symmetries of self-centered focus generate the economic congestion of vast inequality of wealth and income.

339. The logical outcome of a culture of "self" is autocracy, false ideology, and conflict that usurps community, fair trade, and world peace.

340. What is fair is not determined with absolutist judgments and ideologies but by careful attention to nuance and balance, like sailing a boat rather than a megayacht—the illusion stable social distance.

341. We must all find our individual ways to access our moral compass, nature's moral compass.

342. A good start is to look around to see how our fellow creatures are fairing, see if they need help.

343. In an unfair economy, where the rich have too much, there is no such thing as a handout, even though we have been indoctrinated into ideas of bootstraps and false pride.

344. The ego is like bad weather, whether too calm or too windy.

345. The need for help is an opportunity for all to find

nature's balance in motion, with solutions for helpful action in the specific context.

346. There are many ways to try and improve the weather of the soul, to dissipate ego, as evidenced by the massive, often-suspect literature of self-help.

347. The logic of asymmetry suggests that the term "self-help" is misleading.

348. Critical thinking is key to finding out how to stand up for real values, but the use of reason and evidence without empathy—without caring about what others have been through to arrive at their conclusions—will only mislead and weave deeper illusions.

349. A sense of history, of what others have thought and experienced, is vital to the health of nature's moral compass and how we can connect.

350. There is a polarity between mental activity—thinking thoughts—and consciousness *per se*, where soul balance cannot be found without both.

351. Meditation or mindfulness can be helpful in deciding what to do next in life and in carrying out those decisions, if we remember that the objective is not just to "clear the mind," to mention one technique.

352. The polarity between a clear mind or a mind focused on a simple object or mantra at one pole and a mind filled with thoughts means that thoughts and sheer awareness cannot be absolutely separated; the connectivity should be respected in order to receive guidance from a moral compass on the River of Asymmetry.

353. Said another way, all thoughts are consciousness in

the shape of thoughts or words, or music, and so forth, and simple awareness is itself therefore a thought.

ఈ ఆ

Fear not! This humble cabbage, part of nature's bounty, for all its symbolic beauty, and even though it had a core, was not self-aware, nor is the knife, nor the cutting board, nor the table, nor the hand, nor the brain, nor the gut—but the cook? Yes.

354. Does all this polarity mean that everything has some self-conscious identity or soul?

355. By the logic of asymmetry, nature, including the universe, has creativity.

356. The creative River of Asymmetry is everywhere alive and has many polarities but no absolutes.

357. Self-awareness is developed in empathetic, loving relationships with others than ourselves.

358. As much as we might love the humble cabbage, that's not going to cut it (sorry).

359. The atom is not self-aware, but many animals other than humans are, even though they may be sort of dreaming, like us.

360. There is a rhythmic weave that happens where the soul develops in self-referencing repetitive, maze-like cycles woven with others who feel the same way but differently.

361. Who will deny that love is complicated?—with opportunities and boundaries.

362. Love has many manifestations and embodiments.

363. The humble cabbage, turnip or potato, remind us of who needs to be prioritized.

364. We cannot know about poverty without the polarity of personal relationships among different demographics.

365. To build a relationship with "the other" is to cultivate soul consciousness with emotional and intellectual knowledge of the River of Life.

366. To feel the River run through one's soul means there is complexity in being who we are, as the variegated, often-rhythmic, breaking waves and ripples and bubbles

By the Sea Photo Ramona du Houx

over physical, emotional textures remind us that we are alive with self-consciousness.

367. Our hands and feet and the organs of the body, including of course the brain, do not have self-consciousness by themselves.

368. The creativity inferred from the Transformation Proof can develop into the presence of soul that endures with the River of Life, beyond the death of the current, physical body.

369. The panpsychist understanding of universal consciousness does not require the development of complex soul patterns in relationships absolutely everywhere; far from it: such ubiquity of selfhood would mean a collapse into, yes, symmetry.

370. Our differences and distances from each other are

necessary for our humanity, which requires relationships to flourish.

371. The River of Life flows with obstacles and opportunity.

ஐ ஐ

372. The kind of motion favored by fundamental connectivity is always open to opportunities that are highly specific ways for each one of us to find inspiration in the heartbeat of the River, which is love.

373. Every wage and price has a story of the labor in how it came to be, too often with heartbreaking history.

374. Love has a rebalancing agenda that counters the kind of exclusivity that generates oppressive hierarchies of power.

375. The concept of "agents" in economics usurps love—the muted word in a field that purports to define the relationships of desire and affection, agreement and disagreement, among the powers that inform transactions.

376. Nature's love flows in asymmetrical polarity, proactively, though nature does neglect its moral compass.

377. By the logic of asymmetry, we have deduced that there are moral facts indicated by nature's moral compass, which we can share.

378. One of those facts is that nature is nowhere symmetrically homogeneous, as evidenced by all experimental science to date.

379. The Transformation Proof, as previously unfolded with these sutras, tells us that the absence of absolute symmetry means nature, as such, does not act with a single, self-conscious mind.

380. It makes no sense to personify nature and say, for example, "Nature is cruel" or "Nature is loving."

381. But we can deduce that there is a natural love shared by empathetic souls.

382. This deductive panpsychism leads us to a kind of pantheism, where we must conclude that, as mentioned, not only are human animals not the most advanced, hopefully civilized creatures in the universe but there is an ancient, democratic love to be shared throughout many worlds, from beyond "creation" or the Big Bang as we might imagine it.

383. This truth is deep in the soul and clothed in the characters in the stories we share in myth and fiction.

384. The humanities, the arts and music, poetry, film and theater, dance, all bring us this truth when real inspiration is allowed the opportunity to be free.

385. A special affinity for one's god—whether in a monotheistic or pagan or polytheistic context—or an atheistic or agnostic or secular predisposition may bring deeply inspired creativity to be shared in community.

386. It follows, likewise, that absolutely equal opportunity—absolute equality of any kind—is a pure symmetry and therefore lacks context for any opportunities to open up, so it does not happen, nor does absolute freedom have any place to go.

Written in stone tablets—almost.

387. Liberation is found in the relationships of good community, regionally, globally.

388. Equality by the rule of natural law means equal opportunity to develop existing potentials into a good life in a healthy, loving community, locally and beyond.

389. As per sutra 330, in the process of rebalancing the flow of the River of Life, asymmetric democracy fundamentally prioritizes those trapped in the least opportunity, those of us caught in the lowest asymmetry, pressured by society's illusions of absolutes.

390. In the absence of absolute solutions and where the flexibility of nature's asymmetries is low and restricted, pressures build.

391. The blowback is inevitable and difficult to predict, given the subtlety of nature's polarized minds.

392. The more a community provides good chances to those who have had the least opportunity, the healthier it becomes, economically and otherwise.

393. Democratic government is a natural expression of community and not the leftover least of bad options.

394. There is no way but democratic government for communities to become increasingly healthy, wealthy and civilized—that means work and courage, with joy!

395. Democratic government depends on prioritizing opportunities for those who need a chance the most, who are living closest to the symmetries of dead ends.

396. True democracy has asymmetric direction; it does not prioritize aristocracy, oligarchy, billionaires, monarchy, monopolists, or those who need it the least.

397. By prioritizing the disadvantaged, by returning to them their systemically misappropriated wealth, inordinately rich folks will be saved from lapsing into

various dysfunctional forms of neo-feudal infighting throughout succeeding generations.

398. How much net wealth does one need these days for oneself? Will $100,000,000 do it for you? $50,000,000? $25,000,000? No? If not, then we all need a reality check and a hard look at whether the government is doing its job and who is part of one's circle and community.

399. Philanthropy can never match the power for rebalancing change that democratic government can invest.

400. And the upper-middle class? Richard Reeves writes in *Dream Hoarders: How the American Upper Middle Class Is Leaving Everyone Else in the Dust, Why That Is a Problem, and What to Do About It*,

> Americans in the top fifth of the income distribution—broadly, households with incomes above the $112,000 mark—are separating from the rest. This separation is economic, visible in bank balances and salaries. But it can also be seen in education, family structure, health and longevity, even in civic and community life. The economic gap is just the most vivid sign of a deepening class divide . . .
>
> The top fifth of U.S. households saw a $4 trillion increase in pretax income in the years between 1979 and 2013. The combined rise for the bottom 80 percent [four fifths], by comparison, was just over $3 trillion. The gap between the bottom fifth and the middle fifth has not widened at all. In fact, there has been no increase in inequality below the eightieth percentile. All the inequality action is above that line. Income growth has not been

uniform within the top fifth, of course: a third of the income rise went to the top 1 percent alone. But that still left $2.7 trillion for the 19 percent just beneath them. (Brookings Institution Press, Kindle Edition, 2017, pp. 3-7)

401. In other words, everyone in the US economy from 1979 to 2013 got a raise of $7 trillion over what we had been getting in 1979—of which the top fifth got the extra $4 trillion, of which the infamous top one percent got a raise of one third of the top fifth's extra portion; in 2013, folks hustling in the lower four fifths had not opened up any further inequality among themselves since 1979.

402. Of all US economic wealth (household property plus financial assets minus debts), the top one percent's share has risen from about 25 percent since the late 1970s to about 40 percent in 2021 (*Combating Inequality: Rethinking Government's Role*, edited by Olivier Blanchard, Dani Rodrik, The MIT Press, 2021).

403. The widening class divide in the USA since 1979 has been between the top fifth and the lower four fifths of the population, with a mere roomful of individuals taking the lion's share of everyone's shared economy—by our collective moral compass, this spells trouble.

404. Then there is this report, *Survival of the Richest*, published by Oxfam in January 2023, for the world as a whole, with the following press release:

> The richest 1 percent grabbed nearly two-thirds of all new wealth worth $42 trillion created since 2020, almost twice as much money as the bottom

99 percent of the world's population, reveals a new Oxfam report today. During the past decade, the richest 1 percent had captured around half of all new wealth.*

405. These statistics, while extremely revealing, do not of course tell the personal story of US and world poverty and near-poverty.

406. Even though class distinctions among the lower four fifths in the United States have not become more evident, a vast share of national income that should have gone to folks who are struggling—*and without whom there would be no economy*—has gone to the well-off in various proportions.

407. Poverty is caused by us all, even the poor, when they are OK with the inequality that oppresses them.

408. "Knowing your place" in society is an historically commonplace affliction involving various entanglements with degrees and hierarchies of absolutist power.

409. Democracy is the only form of government that works to offset the addiction to absolutes in the long run and short.

410. But in order for democracy to work, we must increase and maintain the political pressure to tax the rich and especially the very rich, or the sickness of addiction will take us all down and totally ruin the planet.

---

*https://www.oxfam.org/en/press-releases/richest-1-bag-nearly-twice-much-wealth-rest-world-put-together-over-past-two-years

The setting sun on the asymmetric water pressure in polarities of turbulence and stillness of this old millrace.

411. Because it is nature's way, democratic action works in finely nuanced ways beyond individual understanding, even to the extent that it can build tension that challenges the people not to succumb to absolutist action—so

that when the time is right, decisive action is effective without being erratic and dictatorial.

412. Because democratic community is nature's way, anything else will inevitably work against the natural environment.

413. Nature may appear to act against itself in many ways, some extremely destructive and cruel—earthquakes, storms, pandemics, predation, you name it—but recall that there is no single, individual self-aware entity that goes by the name of Mother Nature or any other name, like God, that represents the whole and absolutely inclusive group of physical or spiritual systems of any world or universe.

414. But the Transformation Proof's unfurled sails do carry us along with a moral compass that we can call "nature's way" or a natural way to be, more or less.

415. And if the Transformation Proof holds true, what I've called the Asymmetric Pressure Principle predicts a range of behaviors for nature as a whole, including, of course, the economy.

416. The way air and water pressures act along the sails and the hull of a ship requires the areas where pressures impinge—like prices between demand and supply—to be asymmetrically offset and distributed in order for there to be forward progress, where captain and crew must work together.

417. Business managers and investors are involved in hierarchies of power, where special attention is needed to ensure the continuous rebalancing of organizations and economic structures to prioritize participation

Photo Ramona du Houx

All Hands on Deck

in community and in the development of democratic action through workers' unions and climate justice.

418. Making money for its own sake is self-centered symmetry that engenders a loss of soul, as many wealthy individuals may know from close experience, as they work for a better world.

419. Democratic team leadership is required, as ideals of communism, fascism, even "direct democracy" are dysfunctional symmetries; democracy requires the living balance of asymmetric equilibrium in motion and therefore depends on good leadership, where voters check their own moral compass with empathy, reason and evidence.

420. In order to maintain a healthy and efficient military chain of command, balance requires a culture where the defense of true democracy in personal relationships as well as nations is uppermost in the aspirations of all.

421. Addiction creeps into hierarchies of power highly organized for laudable objectives, just as it undermines an anything-goes, let-it-all-hang-out community.

422. A hospitable community that is connected to the past in innovative ways provides places where people of all walks of life can gather and share common respect and enjoyable conversation.

423. The development of quality of place and quality of everyday life requires creativity in the widest sense—from business creativity to the work of creatives and craftspeople, to the character, endurance and quality involved in a job well done—and is a matter of survival for all.

Photo Ramona du Houx

View over the Kennebec River Valley from Robbins Hill, on the Old Canada Road National Scenic Byway, Maine.

ಣ ಬ

424. Absolutism tends to overestimate "soul consciousness" as superior, divinely above the animal body, and to underestimate physical objects as devoid of a connective life force, even as it clings to soulless materialism.

425. While placing consciousness above matter, we disempower it from partaking in the formation of physical objects, and we devalue hands-on work, craftsmanship.

426. Nature's creative flow manifests as art in the environment, not just utilitarian or Darwinian design.

427. Current Darwinian and most scientific theory still does not accept that the landscape is somehow alive.

428. The living landscape is understood in many Native traditions worldwide, where the deeply rooted community can provide a lifeline to rebalance and heal the depredations of addictive technological power.

429. As mentioned, if the River has a nonrandom sense of direction, we are talking about a universal instinct.

430. In the absence of the perfect symmetry of a single omniscient creator deity, organic worlds develop with more or less leadership more or less attuned to the River of Life, the asymmetric environment.

431. The unseen becomes visible in the imagination to inspire words, media, fiction, myth and legend, discoveries in fields of study, even math, inspired by the River.

432. As the heartbeat of the River spreads its waves into the ocean, sky and earth, human animals can be inspired to learn, harmonize, and live with increasing safety among the destructive forces of nature and defuse many dangers.

433. The path of the soul is not discontinued in death; by the logic of asymmetry and the evidence of science, there are no single, isolated life events and no one-off lives lived without creative waves of rhythmic repetition.

434. In life's open-endedness, death is not absolutely final, and physical self-consciousness continues in ways visible and invisible, tangible and intangible, but ever continuing, so we need to get used to the tension and find a home in the polarities of balance, on the River, in the asymmetric environment.

435. The more we take part in nature's inclusive, fundamental sense of direction on the River of Life,

the more the individual, characteristic polarity of the soul in its relationships with others carries us along in multicultural community.

436. The more self-centered we are, the more we lose polarity in relationships and become like an ultimate, angry god, in a self-destructive personal mythology.

437. Omniscience is pure symmetry: there is nothing more for it to know, nothing left over to discover, no avenues into the unknown, no open-endedness; omniscience is an absolute.

438. It is not possible to be omniscient and care about another.

439. Omniscience does not exist.

440. Self-centered singularity self-destructs as it automatically fixates on itself and lack of self-knowledge.

441. The more self-centered one becomes the more one attracts chaos, like a dictator.

442. The economics that preaches "greed is good" is in fact toxic; "shareholder primacy," the self-centered maximization of profits to the exclusion of social responsibility is a pernicious symmetry.

443. The psychological patterns of addiction are invited the more one loses awareness of the way the River prioritizes others, who—perhaps like oneself—do not have the opportunities gained by the more fortunate members of society.

444. Poverty sets up a polarization that attracts natural compensating pressures for balance in the River's flow.

445. The more this natural law is resisted, the more

challenging its eventual and inevitable fulfillment will be; it is further complicated by resistance from both rich and poor, as addictive behavior is subtle and ubiquitous.

446. To feel the River within is to love healthy communities, where variety is appreciated and the imagination is encouraged to help develop exciting and rewarding projects in the marketplace and beyond.

447. Again, we develop soul in natural polarity with one another—with the other.

448. So, one cannot cure oneself first without caring for others; the cure is in the caring, a healing flow.

449. We do not develop strength of soul by loving ourselves first; exclusive self-love is low asymmetry that builds counter-pressures.

450. Personal problems can often be traced back to lack of understanding of other people and cultures.

451. Self-esteem alone is not self-sustaining.

452. The slightest good, solid, shared accomplishment can be a contribution that no ego boost can match.

453. The cultivation of self-empowerment backs up on the individual in forms of victimhood and scapegoating.

454. "Me-first" culture has led to a disintegration of community that fuels racism, bigotry, authoritarian rule, and the eventual depletion and destruction of markets through erratic, dictatorial behavior.

455. The democratic impulse is instinctive in us all—in our stories, our folk tales and daily actions—and develops character the more we act to help the cultural environment of the River of Life, the Tao.

456. Looking outward to another soul in mutual polarity, to listen, to help out if needed, opens the way for us to identify with individual personality, with wit and humility, free of unhealthy dependency.

457. Looking too much inwards to figure out who we are can congest the soul with loss of identity.

458. By looking and listening to improve the quality of life of the community as an ongoing theme in work and play, we avoid becoming overly polarized in soul, stuck in a fixed position of being, where life becomes a sort of cliché, a false independence.

459. Nor do we want to be all polarities, godlike, all "balanced," disintegrating in a symmetry of "oneness."

460. Male or female or in-between, a key to avoidance of absolutism is to lose oneself somewhat, a kind of risk, like making a fool of oneself, in recognition of empathy.

461. There is no absolute male, no absolute female, and no pure gender neutrality.

462. The absence of absolute femininity or masculinity does not require that both polarities be identified in the soul; there are many ways just to be male, female.

463. The absence of absolutes in gender means that gender polarity is naturally subtle and creative, whether male or female or LGBTQ+, to the extent that many currents and counter-currents can develop one's balance and personality in relationships.

464. No one should be pressured or expected to know or decide their gender, especially at an early age.

465. Gender polarity is a way for diversity to develop

naturally; without sexual polarity, manifesting variously, life would not even be bland, as it would not exist at all.

466. Love is the answer; it is also the question that invites.

☙ ❧

467. Authoritarianism suppresses and abuses questioning and honest sexuality.

468. The dictatorial leaders of China today promote Confucius to provide cover for the lack of a moral compass in their paradoxically materialist communism and to head off social counter-currents that might lead to chaos when their self-centered polarization conjures its demons; they correctly suspect that capitalist materialism is too narrow a guide for the people.

469. The emperors of China believed they had to get the blessing of the powers of nature in order to rule.

470. Confucianism led the people with unbalanced polarity in a ritualized and rigid, patrician, male-dominated hierarchy, in the belief that this leads to virtue through self-improvement.

471. The sage Mencius redirected early Confucianism to teach the subordination of the ruler to the people, through the cultivation of benevolence, merging with Taoist naturalism, emphasizing education.

472. Understanding the polarities of the Tao, we can learn to live more safely on this planet, especially confronted with the way the climate has been abused and the way it is responding with unleashed pressures in the attempt to regain balance and direction.

473. We need continuously to develop awareness of the nature of change.

474. Change is not just a paradox, and all relativism ultimately fails to describe it.

475. Relativism clings to symmetrical randomness and thereby merges with judgmental absolutism.

476. Change sometimes trends in a way that can appear to be heading for a climactic, ultimate destination, but in the absence of absolutes, the Tao is already tending away, pressured by the truth of impossibilities.

477. This is a creative, living, kind of behavior that functions like it is aware in diverse and evolving ways, rather than like a machine or the so-called blind watchmaker of current Darwinian lore.

478. Consciousness is as subtle as the creative continuum of the River of Life; in its vastness throughout the universe, it does not need to ride in a spaceship to be part of the planet.

479. The humble asymmetries of science can discover worlds within worlds.

480. Yoganomics is about the empathetic connection between the asymmetric economy and the time-honored idea of Yin and Yang, with reason and evidence.

481. Focused on a Platonic misunderstanding of soul, we have long underestimated the natural, material world and banished the mind to invisibility with the soul.

482. But many of our ancestors and people today hold beliefs that respect inanimate things as worthy of life—the mountains are alive, the rocks are alive, the land lives.

483. In the polarities of nature, there are what humans have called gods, muses, and spirits who have inspired tales that modern societies relegate to mythology and outdated belief systems, but beliefs come round again in patterns that never repeat exactly.

484. The tree, like the soul, might sheds its leaves, and

the leaves continue into the environment without the self-awareness of the soul, but alive in the process of conscious change.

485. The search to locate awareness, self-consciousness or one's mind exclusively within the confines of the nervous system or the body will become moribund, in the absence of focus on connections to one's social and cultural relationships and beyond into the wider environment.

486. The logic of asymmetry supports the scientific approach of advancement with mistakes, using the working, questioning hypothesis, and so forth.

487. The purposeful acceptance and gathering of information by process of error, curiosity, humility, and doubt is an ongoing revolution in human history.

488. An unassuming sense of self—of not thinking one is "the one" or that one must become "the one"—is fairly impossible without comedy with the ability to laugh at oneself, reflected in fiction, with characters that allow us to practice being in the shoes of others.

489. Economics has suffered from a lack of empathy.

490. It is vital for students of economics (and many other fields of study) to have knowledge of history and the humanities—to know how their discipline developed—to avoid becoming indoctrinated.

491. As demonstrated, students have been systematically ensconced in ideas of free-market capitalism that assume fundamental symmetry, often powered by math, with naïve economism or 101ism becoming cult-like.

492. Because math is currently based on symmetry and paradox, it has lots of trouble describing the asymmetries of the economy, except through statistics.

493. Math currently makes the study of that part of nature where asymmetry is lowest (appearing very symmetrical) look like "hard science," until further and more profound discoveries raise the importance of the fundamental asymmetry already at the surface in the social sciences.

494. The ability to look into the economic and social conditions of people's livelihoods—to put ourselves in their shoes without intrusion—in order to right the imbalances of our vast inequality is potentially transformative.

495. We need an understanding of natural law and the empathy to deal with the challenges that capitalism can present to democracy.

496. There is nothing intrinsically democratic about capitalism.

497. The freedoms that develop through asymmetric democracy allow capitalism to happen, but capitalism has developed under the dictatorship of communist China, for example, while democracy has been suppressed.

☙ ❧

498. Artificial intelligence (AI) lacks the complex, maze-like polarity developed in naturally creative and open relationships of love, so it's socially dependent.

499. AI will remain artificial and dependent on guidance,

for good or ill, depending on the community and culture, the quality of the data it finds, and the degree of asymmetry fundamentally assumed.

500. The more it feeds off its omniscience, the more pernicious and ultimately self-destructive AI becomes.

501. Asymmetries of natural law—as in the law of the land and judicial systems—have been monopolized and usurped by religion in many ways, with claims that our sense of guilt and our human conscience are the gift of a moral compass from an omniscient god.

502. As we get our instinctive and time-honored law rightly credited—a morality that comes through nature's River of Life in every culture—we are in the process of healing the community and the planet.

503. The continued development of the rule of law must involve an improved understanding of its deep connection with the forces of nature and environmental justice.

504. To insist on a fixed, "originalist" interpretation of a constitution is a destabilizing symmetry that will destroy a nation, unless the constitution and the law are liberated and allowed to live, breathe and flow with the awareness of the River.

505. Sutra 48 referenced the way the extremely low asymmetry of repeating patterns of units (like algorithms, binary code, or mathematical sequences) requires the presence of a creative continuity—so AI is like the cabbage, when it comes to having a moral compass.

506. AI should not be allowed to usurp the rule of law, where the soul of agreement is the key to civilization.

507. Capitalism has fueled destructive monopolistic coercion, sidetracked our moral compass and confused prices, even as democracy has allowed it to develop advances in civilization.

508. Monopoly and monopsony (where there is, for example, only one buyer or employer, who can therefore set the price or wage) misuse democracy and the individual votes of the people against the people.

509. Monopoly and monopsony usurp free agreement, whether in contracts, contract law, or a simple handshake.

510. Healthy competition is fine within the rules and law, but it is not essential to a free and civilized market economy; transactions happen because of agreement—there is no economy without agreement.

511. We can remove haggling and competition, and we can, of course, still agree on a price and move forward with projects.

512. What connects us is more fundamental than what divides us.

513. Monopoly and monopsony suppress competition along with free agreement.

514. Markets do not depend on competition—they do depend on cooperation.

☙ ☙

515. There is a polarity of demand for balance, to be supplied in the River of Asymmetry.

516. It's a demand brought about in the absence of

absolutes—it functions in a continuous current of activity, requesting, begging, imploring, suggesting . . .

517. Against this demand for balance in motion is an adverse counter-current of demand—denying, oppressing, ignoring, grasping with greed for the eternally missing object of the particular addiction in some degree of advancement.

518. If the people demand good democratic government, it will eventually be supplied to them, along with healthier markets.

519. Without systems such as ranked-choice voting and the provision of continuously improved opportunities for people to vote and be truly represented, our markets will fail, and so will civilization.

520. Libertarians who want the power to deprive community of its ability to join forces in guiding good government are asking for monopoly and monopsony, along with depleted, congested and chaotic markets—and war, consciously or not.

521. Demand for the simplest object is always moving somewhere else; there is no fundamental tendency towards perfect equilibrium at a perfectly true price, so the people need to manage their markets with the empathy of good business, not like libertarian control freaks.

522. All transactions are made, all orders are signed at prices along the way to the next temporary marker or signpost in a changing flow.

523. In fact, as mentioned, markets *must tend away* from the nonexistence of any perfect equilibrium symmetry.

524. We need an economics based on the value of nature's fundamental moral compass, not the vicissitudes of our worst impulses and nature's disruptions.

525. The attempt to encourage equilibrium symmetry, even as natural forces will inevitably work to avoid such an impossible absolute from happening, will generate chaotic market conditions, jumbled with booms and busts, with the potential for long-term recessions and worse.

526. Demand for absolutes is supplied with unstable conditions, where narcissistic personalities rise to power, and the worship of religious purity and ideological perfection bedevils the addiction with chaos.

527. Economic growth and productivity must be measured in terms of real value, with the prioritization of the numbers on nature's moral compass.

528. Otherwise the economy will flounder in heavy seas and chaos, time and again.

529. The media must routinely use and publicize the numbers generated by the impressive body of work worldwide to reconfigure outdated and dangerous measures of national product, income, wealth, productivity, and growth—for the improvement of a valued life of real individuals, growing the community (not just "growing an economy" of markets) in the rehabilitation of the planet.

530. The degrees of institutional addiction to fantasies of absolutes harbor paranoias of conspiracy and desires for a godlike leader who loves with omniscience and can handle absolute power to resolve the impossible; this is

the danger in the worship of conflicted gods, dictators, even philosopher kings, as well as the adulation of celebrities and characters imagined, while demonizing those who can help.

531. Likewise, when we hear claims of "exceptionalism," we can understand this as ego; history happens in patterns of development with enough rhythm to learn from the past and know that there are no such exceptions.

532. Being a fundamental instinct, democracy is not exceptional or new; it gets renewed like the Magna Carta and is known to have arisen to acceptance in government in one form or other, from ancient India to ancient Greece and Rome, to the roots of the oldest surviving European parliaments, the Icelandic Althing and the Tynwald of the Isle of Man.

533. The Iroquois Confederacy was famously studied by Benjamin Franklin and the US Founders to see how democracy might be reapplied in the American colonies.

534. Good leadership leads like the River, and brings democratic systems to the forefront and tries to maintain and improve them, so it is widespread in the development of humanity, in spite of reversals.

535. Like the markets of the asymmetric economy, democracy is not self-righting, self-regulating, or maintenance-free.

536. The blowback from absolutist fixations can destroy democratic cultures.

Photo Ramona du Houx

Sails

537. Good leadership in the community does not supply shoddy goods with the excuse that it's what people want, nor should it pander to ego.

538. In a healthy economy, people can afford quality—and healthcare is universally available as a natural human

right, not an exception reserved for those who can pay.

539. In a healthy economy, taxation is sufficiently progressive to deal with institutional addiction.

540. Unfair taxation, where low and lower-middle incomes are taxed when they shouldn't be, and the wealthy are taxed so they hardly notice (except as regards their image and ego) leads to mass incarceration.

541. The more the usurped potential and real productivity of the people—especially those without a roof over their heads, without healthcare, without sufficient goods and services, investment in education—are left out of measures of national income, the more their contributions are disqualified and unaccounted for, leaving impoverished and misleading statistics.

542. For generations, the national income of the US economy has grown, while the vast majority of individual incomes have fallen short, stagnated, or never been received at all, leaving people destitute: Where did the money go?—where else could it go than to those who have too much.

543. People's lost share of national wealth went to members of society in error, whether they wished it or not—an error deeply felt via the River of Asymmetry, not always clearly identified, but an error that needs correction with nature's moral compass, or people will naturally rise up in waves of rebellion.

544. Social injustice cannot be kept hidden forever.

545. The rule of law in many countries and traditions recognizes that ownership is not absolute; no one owns the River of Life, the Tao.

546. Ownership is responsibility to the River of Life with a measure of personal power; this power is all too often abused, leading to the *de facto* usurpation of livelihoods, systemic racial injustice, the destabilization of communities and the ruin of entire economies.

547. While some wealthy individuals may understand the risks of ownership power, personally and for the economy, too many lose track, as they weaken and succumb to the competitive demands of their increasingly closed and vulnerable inner circles.

548. Money, however defined, relieves many kinds of tension when it relieves poverty, and in ways that mindfulness and stress management techniques cannot.

549. The universal instinct is to help nature and have a healthy life along the River, a spiritual exercise in itself.

550. Financial relief to the poor and those struggling to make ends meet is not a handout; it is help in freeing up the universal instinct to help out and should first and foremost be in the form of direct transfers of money to them personally—a long overdue return on their investment in an economy that would crumble without them.

551. The poor and lower-income individuals have carried the burden of a heavily lopsided, intensely polarized economy—they stand between us and the collapse of our democracy.

552. The rich, not so much.

553. The centuries-old claim that transfers of funds to the poor are a disincentive to work is the psychological projection of elites for whom work is optional.

554. It's a moral fact that an honest day's work is a natural human instinct.

555. Those who carry the enduring stress of never having enough money—nor properly valued work—should be more respected in the community and among lawmakers than the "gods" of business and their currently obscene remuneration.

556. People who handle the stress of poverty, living on the edge day to day, should be praised and rewarded for their fortitude; reparations for their usurped wealth should be provided to them; they should be looked to with respect and for advice on dealing with tension and perseverance.

557. It is well established that stress can sicken and kill the body; the same is true of the body of the economy.

558. Markets flow best when ample resources are channeled to free up opportunity where it is least available, taking a risk in the process.

559. There is a kind of wall or threshold through which one inevitably passes when the tension of poverty and hardship breaks, when one's income becomes sufficient.

560. After a while, on the other side of this wall, the relief can itself build automatically with subtle power, based on differential pressure; if one is born on the easy side of the wall, the relief is even more automatic, as surely as the poverty remains on the other side, and well-heeled soldiers sally forth to lobby and collect.

561. This power relationship of poverty-dependent relief can be deduced from the logic of asymmetry, because the River runs in polarity through the wall.

562. Despite progress in economics, too many are still in denial about the wall of power round the castles, even though it is so obvious.

563. The profound inability to act to rebalance the economy, when effective tools are right at hand, is evidence of the weakness of addiction.

564. History has repeatedly shown how this wall caves in the violence of revolutions and war, for better or worse, but always too late.

565. And now we have the blowback of climate change, as nature's River of Asymmetry attempts to rebalance the environment, after the adverse pressures of a polluted global economy.

566. This is not a self-righting, self-regulating system, where we can stand aside and opt out; Mother Nature needs our help to help save our best tendencies from our worst—she is neither all-powerful nor omniscient.

567. We can all find ways to help in even the slightest everyday actions that accumulate to bring rebalancing effects along the River, with a little humor and wit—that goes a long way, too.

568. There is an intangible sense of entitlement that threatens to become palpable in everyday actions of the rich and which provides fodder for comedians.

569. There is no balance without comedy, as in a word like "yoganomics," if ever so slight.

570. So this is by no means a perfect or complete treatment of the Transformation Proof, but it is more than enough for now.

The Author

Born in Los Angeles, California, Paul Cornell du Houx grew up among several Western countries. Graduating from Winchester College in the UK, he attended Amherst College in Massachusetts, where he majored separately in economics and French.

Photo Ramona du Houx

His honors thesis identified the aesthetic mysticism in the works of Gustave Flaubert. This led to his early attempts to bring cross-cultural insights to clarify a crisis some economists saw in the utilitarian way mainstream theory was moving. He decided to investigate the marketplace firsthand, rather than take the well-worn academic path that one day would lead the world economy into the Great Recession and largely unprepared into the 2020 pandemic. Clearly, capitalism had long gone begging for something more than money.

While looking for answers, Cornell du Houx wrote currency reports for the MSA consultancy newsletter in the London Square Mile, audited companies for PwC, studied law at the Inns of Court, sold computers to a wide variety of companies, and with his patented improvements on an electrical connector got involved in a start-up. The author's first gathering of sutras under the *Yoganomics* portmanteau was in 1979.

Eventually, Cornell du Houx developed a math that lets us read the ethics of natural law within the environment, described with illustrative stories and essays in *Unicycle, the Book of Fictitious Symmetry and Nonrandom Truth, or the Panpsychist Asymmetry of Nature's Democratic Pi.*

In 2019 he rewrote *Yoganomics*, retaining the ancient and succinct style of the sutra, to further apply the new ideas of the Transformation Proof found in *Unicycle.*

Somewhere along the line, he wrote *What the Farmer Told the Bard, a Novel of Erotic Panpsychism* (2020), involving runes encoded in a Shakespeare monument and some pagan deities from the Bard's comedies.

In 1991 Ramona and Paul settled with their children in Maine. The publication of books, art, and the news magazine *Maine Insights* led to founding the Solon Center for Research and Publishing (501c3) and EOPA Code Blue Water Solutions (501c4).

The Solon Center's Gallery Fukurou, at 20 Main Street, Rockland, Maine, opened to the public in 2018 (GalleryFukurou.com).

The independently founded project Elected Officials to Protect America (ProtectingAmerica.net) joined with the Solon Center to combat climate change, with the help and leadership of military veterans.

It is the author's hope that the sense of a deep democracy in nature, which inspired Native American communities and merged with the U.S. Founders' Enlightenment vision of natural law, will help bring hearts and minds together in time.

Appendix: Definitions of Symmetry and Asymmetry

Emily Cornell du Houx

Asymmetry is defined by Webster's New World College Dictionary as "lack of symmetry." Webster's definition of symmetry is "similarity of form or arrangement on either side of a dividing line or plane," and "correspondence of opposite parts in size, shape, and position."

At first sight, symmetry is easy to find wherever we look. Your window might be a rectangle divided into four panes—though each pane will frame a different part of the view out the window. So the view through the symmetrical window would be asymmetrical. Technically speaking, symmetry is often described as happening where some operation leaves the object in question unchanged in some way—even though that changing operation is connected to it. Symmetry and paradox often go hand in hand.

The window has symmetry about the vertical axis, for example, dividing it in two. This can be described as a reflection about the vertical axis or a translation where the two left-hand panes would look the same if they were slid over somehow to replace the right-hand panes. Of course we know that such a theoretical operation in practice may not work out so simply. The pane would have to be removed, and the glass of one pane might be cut to fit exactly the original square in the window and might not fit so well if reused to replace the opposite square, especially with some warping and weathering of the frame. So although "symmetry," loosely speaking, once we start looking for it, can be sighted just about everywhere, from the flowers to the leaves to the blades of grass to the sharpest technologies, when we take a closer look—or when we stand back—things can get complicated and less than ideally symmetrical.

There are many handy categories of symmetry that we learn about in math class. For example, the symmetry of repetition or translation, which one finds in a ladder or a repeating series, where any rung or unit appears to be translatable to the next position without having to undergo any change. There is point symmetry at the center of a circle, where we set the point of our compass in order to draw the circumference. The point is symmetrical as it does not seem to change in any essential way—even as the compass needle turns in the paper. Then there is the symmetry of a flat surface that does not appear to have any variations. Wherever we are on the surface, it is the same as any other place with respect to any other place (or even with respect to some coordinates). The surface is entirely homogeneous. This raises more than a few questions and paradoxes right away—like where are we? Are we anywhere at all?

There are symmetrical equations in math that are used in what has been called a "language of symmetry" or group theory. The question remains as to whether any of this "symmetry" is really sufficiently symmetrical to merit the term, even—or especially—when it is in the psyche of the mathematician in the guise of "pure math."

In order to address these and other related questions, we qualify symmetry with such terms as "absolute," "pure," or "perfect" and use them in this way interchangeably for variety. Here we consider "absolute" or "perfect" symmetry as having such uniformity as to give rise to no differences, changes, or variations, whether through a given operation or not. Anything else is asymmetric.

Selected Bibliography

Blyth, Mark. *Austerity: The History of a Dangerous Idea*. Oxford University Press, 2015.

Brown, Clair. *Buddhist Economics: An Enlightened Approach to the Dismal Science*. London: Bloomsbury Press, 2017

Chalmers, David, and Andy Clark. "The Extended Mind." *Analysis* 58: 1: (1998): 7–19. Also: www.philosophy.ed.ac.uk/people/clark/pubs/TheExtendedMind.pdf.

Close, Frank. *Lucifer's Legacy: The Meaning of Asymmetry*. Mineola: Dover Publications, 2014.

Crair, Ben. "The Fishy Mystery of Lake Malawi." *Smithsonian Magazine*, March 2019. https://www.smithsonianmag.com/science-nature/mystery-lake-malawi-180971442/.

Florida, Richard. *The Rise of the Creative Class: And How It's Transforming Work, Leisure, Community and Everyday Life*. New York: Basic Books, 2019.

Fox, Justin. *The Myth of the Rational Market: A History of Risk, Reward, and Delusion on Wall Street*. New York: Harper, 2011.

Keynes, John Maynard. *The General Theory of Employment, Interest, and Money*. San Diego: Harcourt, Brace & World, 2016.

Mazzucato, Mariana. *The Value of Everything: Making and Taking in the Global Economy*. London: Penguin, 2019.

Piketty, Thomas. *Capital in the Twenty-First Century*. Cambridge: Harvard University Press, 2017.

Reich, Robert B. *Aftershock: The Next Economy and America's Future*. New York: Vintage Books, 2013.

Sennett, Richard. *The Craftsman*. New Haven & London: Yale University Press, 2008.

Smith, Fran. "The Addicted Brain." *National Geographic* Sept. 2017. https://www.nationalgeographic.com/magazine/2017/09/the-addicted-brain/.

Smolin, Lee. *Time Reborn: From the Crisis in Physics to the Future of the Universe*. Boston, New York: Houghton Mifflin Harcourt, 2014.

Wilhelm, Richard and Cary F. Baynes, translators. *The I Ching or Book of Changes*. Princeton: Princeton University Press, 1967.

Wu, Tim. *The Attention Merchants: The Epic Scramble to Get Inside Our Heads*. New York: Vintage, 2017.

www.ingramcontent.com/pod-product-compliance
Lightning Source LLC
LaVergne TN
LVHW052111090426
835512LV00037B/2555